Thank You to All the Sneaky Links

Kristin Lyon

BookLeaf Publishing

India | USA | UK

Presentation by *BookLeaf Publishing*

Web: www.bookleafpub.com

E-mail: info@bookleafpub.com

ISBN: 9789360948306

First edition 2024

*To everyone who makes my life more real.
For all the feelings and the inspirations.
For making me want to be better and
forcing me to accept myself. And especially
to the best man: my pyr Bubba.*

PREFACE

These poems may or may not be about my dog.

comfort (and joy)

He's tucked in, barely moving.
Watching him inhale softly.His lips gently part
as the air escapes.
An overwhelming peace melts over me;
watching him sleep like this.
I've given him everything.
I've given him the peace to be in this moment
and it's one of the best things I've done with my
life.
The why that I'm here.
I've never had that and never chased that. It just
seemed like something unattainable for me.
In big ways I don't see it. But here on the living
room floor I'm so complete and satisfied.
I don't want him to know that I've done this all
for him.
I just hope he feels a fraction of the joy he brings
me.

swimming

2

he exhales. so slow it seems like time has
stopped. and I shudder. taking in every
centimeter. each it's own bite, caress. hollow
bones, levitation, a shiver, a vise. circles then.
spinning my head. I want to be self conscious
but it's too perfect. abdomen rises, tense. eye
contact, I avoid it in the real world, but this, this
is a waterfall. looking down, muffled sound.
imagining it now takes me right there.
swimming. experiences I don't want to live
without. shallow waters but some of the most
cherished memories. you, you deserve the world.
you gave that to me. even now, hours after, I
melt, choppy breath. exhale.

soulmates

If my soul is wicked, would my soul mate be wicked too? Should we complement or contrast? Who am I looking for? Feeling in the dark. And would I know if it hit me? Square between the four eyes, on the 5th eye, like a battering ram. It must be more subtle. A vine pulsing down synapses to my core. Or maybe it's not a feeling at all, only a knowing, a longing. My lungs and my knees have been true through the years. Maybe it's one of them. I've held multitudes of joy and quick thunderstrikes of pain. My soul in pinks and greens soars free and wild. I'm climbing a mountain, daring to keep up. And there I see a glimmer of my soul's mate. She's staring up at me from a cold glassy alpine lake. Familiar eyes. And she whispers, "don't ever be afraid to jump."

Tin Man

4

White matter or gray matter
It doesn't matter
What it's telling me I don't believe
If it's wrong why can't I keep away the grin?
Is it possible to crash and not get hurt?
Maybe the pain would be worth the moments.
To be scared and do it anyway.
It's nothing.
But it's actually everything to me and that's
where the danger begins.
I'm balancing on the cliff's edge and I've taken
off the harness.
I'm chasing a feeling.
I'm following something else.

check-in

Hey
Are you OK?
They told me the reason this can't work is
because someone always wants more.
Someone always gets hurt.
I assumed, as I do, that it was me.
I would be hurt.
But what if I was wrong, and it was you?
I can be selfish, so that checks out.
What do you want that I'm not giving you?
What do you need that I don't have?
Are you going to be OK in the end?
I don't mind being hurt, I deserve it.
But I do not want to hurt you.

Orion's belt

An inky darkness so devoid of light
I forget what position my body is oriented
And incandescent bodies dot the sky
I want so badly to share this with you
Because sometimes you make my body
incandescent too
The wind is blowing softly, the air that escapes
my lips is visible
Somewhere off, I wonder how far, an owl calls,
"who cooks for you?"
My body, wrapped in down, still disoriented in
space
I tell myself I'll get a better camera so you can
see
But it's the night as a whole
Filling my lungs with this air
Watching each star glitter
Pointing out the constellations and humming so
freely
A picture could never express how deeply the
sky grounds me

I usually love the sky

My body is not at its best
My eyes are damp and down
The feeling underneath my chest
Right before the tears fall
Shaky, unsure, panic
And I'm so angry at myself
The idiot romantic
So many signs
I made up in my head
So many times
I ignored what everyone said
And I knew too
It's only physical
This thing between me and you
Is that why I'm aching
Or I'm wishing we were more
When I didn't give you anything
Besides chemistry we can't ignore
So I'm selfish
And I'm to blame
I should have been honest
And figured out my own endgame
When now it's too late
And I'm crushed, I'm upset
Let me feel all my feels
This is our sunset

Waveforms and Frequencies

"I know you love waveforms"

vibrations

proof of life and proof of living

the one you see

the other you feel

I don't always trust my feelings

dig deeper, breathe deeper

trust myself deeper

emit those vibrations I hope to receive

not just alive

living

Stay Away

I'm in rough terrain
I need to find the way out
I dont want your ghost distracting me
I'll never say anything
Just jump right back in
And fall off the edge again
I always make the same mistake
I never was a good listener
And something about you makes me ignore
the usual signs
It's not really there but I want it so bad
I'll move all the flags while chasing you
I need to stop
But I won't stop
That's why I'm asking please
Stay away this time

the game

you came so fast
once you saw me
and I know it's part of your game
but I definitely folded
and I'm back all in like before
you have something
that I can't say no to
that I'm not strong enough to quit on my own
I want every piece, every jewel, every flaw
show me your everything
I'm playing a game too
but the one I'm lying to is myself
if I could pause time while your arms are around
me
your eyes gazing upon me
your lips drinking me in
I would forever win this game

The Fish Box

Sits on a shelf with the most important things
Not large but not miniature either
And it looks antique
What does it mean?
What does it hold?
I could have opened the box
But most everyone has heard of Pandora
This is one thing I don't want to risk ruining
Plus I like to imagine
What might be inside
A tooth, some pictures, chewing gum
What if it plays a song?
Letters to ex lovers, DNA, currency
Let my imagination run free
And maybe when it's over
And we're talking about regrets and missed
opportunities
I'll wonder aloud
What's in the box?

Sisters

12

My sister was always better at everything
She's faster, stronger, smarter
More beautiful
What I have is that I'm deliriously delusionally
happy
And wild and free
I hope she feels that way sometimes too

bestfriends

Deep down, I probably knew
Something was wrong, distant
And I forgave that, for what?
Years of my youth gone missing
But then I felt safe I felt proud
I also wanted to know
What this was, what it meant

Like the first time we met
A squeeze between my ribs
But
This nerve is new
Not ready
Stay here breathe slow
Back then it was giddy
Fluttering and light
Unsettled but easy
Stay here breathe slow
Nerves and energy rattle around my skull
Only a peaceful blank look shows
Will you know

It's different than what I imagined
Better maybe

So comfortable
Too comfortable?

And secrets were hiding
From me and from you too
And I want to be angry
I want to scream
For all the youth we've lost

But I love how strong and independent I've
become
And I love to see you, happy and free
You sing along to music again
The giddy, the fluttering, the light in your eyes is
back

So now I want to be angry
How did I not see
How far we slipped away from ourselves
Is that growth, when you are back sliding

I can't be angry
I can only be proud
We're here
We're surviving
We came out on top

KJ

15

I can't get a good look at her eyes because they
are too focused.
Imagine if she focused those eyes on me.
The way she moves,
It's like poetry.
Strong and light
Rotating through the hips.
It's like she can fly.
Do I want to be with her or do I want to fly like
her?
I think it's part both.
I want both.

girl's girl

I'm a girl's girl
to a fault I think
I'd need more than one hand
to count the women I've sent to you
no claim, no jealousy
there's enough love for everyone right?

ok maybe a little jealousy
so maybe it's better if we share
or do I just want to know you had your choice
and out of all the tiramisu, buttercream, pavlova
you chose me
and I'm not as much of a girl's girl as I seem

and he's back hooking up too
it's messing with me
but not how I originally suspect
I'm mad for her
she's the one who's going to get hurt in the end
while he is going to move on like a tornado
never looking back to see what he's torn apart
hopefully she's playing him too
and I can stop worrying about her being caught
in the path
destruction

I wish it upon no one
but why do I feel the need to protect them
why can't I just stay safely away

a tiny fire

forcing my heart on paper
taking the pen and letting it bleed
I'm more damaged than I realize
broken tortured mind
here I thought I was settled, joyous, fine even
and somewhere I'm smoldering away
project and protect
letting no one in
I want to let you read these so bad
you tried more than once
the closest anyone's ever been to my depth
and it terrifies me
I'm shaking as I furiously scribble the words on
the page
blood mixed with salt mixed with ink mixed
with more tears
I can't have you find this side of me
even though it could be the most beautiful thing
to let you in
a wave of serenity but more likely the
earthquake complete with aftershocks
I'm curious now, how you will do
if I could let you uncover the monster

calm my anxious mind

19

I want to run into your arms right now
Let you hold me, ground me
I'm not going to cry, we're not there yet
Just tuck my face into the place where it fits on
the side of your chest
And take a few deep breaths
While you hold my shoulders with one hand
My head with the other
Don't let go yet
Feel the perfection that life sometimes can be
And gather strength to go out and face it again

Mixmaster

I love the love
They all feed me so much dopamine
Call me Walter White
A chemist exploring bonds
And looking for a little explosion
Provoking it
His touch, his smell
His lips
There's no question unasked
But I know almost nothing about him
A best friend
But also a stranger
He bounces around the room
Kinetic energy
But I am the nucleus
He revolves around

da Gama

The one I need to explore
Is myself
Real things
What I want
What I want to be
I haven't really planned my future
I've been too focused on the present
Is it OK to wander aimlessly
As long as I'm happy
Take some time
Alone
And discover the lioness
Can I be an artist
How do I move my body
What I want to learn
Which ways I want to grow
Who I'm meant to touch
What fires am I meant to start
And will I do it
Continue to expand
Stretch across the sky
Voluminous, polychromatic, opalescent

After I leave

After I leave
Keep me this way in your mind
A friend
An open heart
I would do anything
To make you feel seen
Loved

manifestation

1/24/24 0336

333
i wished for you
but idk if that's even what i want
? best case scenario
maybe maybe maybe
when 333 comes again
i'll think of something else

1/29/24 1734

<But I never do>

9 789360 948306